"Guide My Pen"

The Poems of Phillis Wheatley

Greg Roza

ROSEN CENTRAL
PRIMARY SOURCE™

THE ROSEN PUBLISHING GROUP, INC., NEW YORK

Published in 2004 by The Rosen Publishing Group, Inc.
29 East 21st Street, New York, NY 10010

Editor: Scott Waldman
Book Design: Michelle Innes
Photo Researcher: Rebecca Anguin-Cohen
Series Photo Researcher: Jeff Wendt

Photo Credits: Cover (left), title page, p. 14 Courtesy of the Massachusettes Historical Society;
cover (right) illustration © Debra Wainwright/The Rosen Publishing Group; p. 6 © Corbis;
pp. 10, 22 © North Wind Picture Archives; pp. 18, 29 Library of Congress Prints and
Photographs Division; p. 30 Library of Congress Rare Books and Special Collections Division;
p. 31 Private Collection/The Bridgeman Art Library; p. 32 Library of Congress Manuscript Division

First Edition

Library of Congress Cataloging-in-Publication Data

Roza, Greg.
    Guide my pen : the poems of Phillis Wheatley / Greg Roza.— 1st ed.
    p. cm. — (Great moments in American history)
    Summary: Poetess and freed slave Phillis Wheatley writes a poem
celebrating General George Washington's leadership in the American
Revolution, and is invited to his camp to meet the future president.
    ISBN 0-8239-4381-X (lib. bdg.)
    1. Wheatley, Phillis, 1753-1784—Juvenile literature. 2. Poets,
American—Colonial period, ca. 1600-1775—Biography—Juvenile
literature. 3. Slaves—United States—Biography—Juvenile literature.
4. African American poets—Biography—Juvenile literature. [1.
Wheatley, Phillis, 1753-1784. 2. Poets, American. 3. Slaves. 4. African
Americans—Biography. 5. Women—Biography.] I. Title. II. Series.

    PS866.W5Z693 2004
    811'.1—/dc21
                                                            2003005996

Manufactured in the United States of America

CONTENTS

Preface

When the slave-trading ship *Phillis* sailed in to Boston Harbor from Africa on July 11, 1761, few people took notice. Slaves were a common sight everywhere in the colonies. In fact, most of the business, as well as the social life, in the colonies depended on the cruel system of slavery. African men, women, and children were taken against their will from their homes and forced to work for white colonists. Slaves were not paid for their work, and they were not treated well in most cases. Many of the colonial leaders who wanted independence from England—even George Washington—owned slaves.

A young girl on the *Phillis* was bought by the Wheatleys of Boston and named after the ship—Phillis Wheatley. Phillis learned to read and write English within sixteen months of coming to America. Yet no one knew that she would grow up to become a great writer. Phillis would spend the rest of her life working hard to accomplish greatness in a difficult world.

Phillis's master, John Wheatley, and his wife, Susannah, encouraged Phillis to read and write. Teaching slaves such important skills was almost unheard of in colonial America. After publishing her first poem at age fourteen, Phillis became famous from Boston, Massachusetts, to London, England. Phillis did many great things to prove that black people were the equals of those who made them slaves. She was the first African American to publish a book. She was also the first African American woman to make money from her writing.

Phillis was a slave, a poet, and a patriot. She loved her country as much as any American citizen. Yet she was torn between two worlds— that of white colonists and that of black slaves—never feeling completely a part of either.

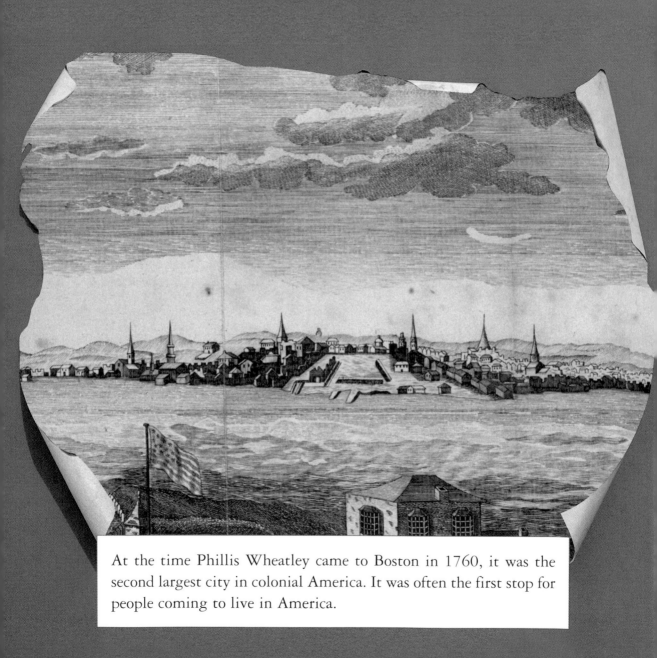

At the time Phillis Wheatley came to Boston in 1760, it was the second largest city in colonial America. It was often the first stop for people coming to live in America.

6

Chapter One

BACK IN BOSTON

August 2, 1773

Phillis Wheatley had been in London for over a month. Stepping off the boat in Boston Harbor, however, she felt as if she had never left. The docks still had the same familiar sounds: gulls squawking, water lapping, chains clanking. The thrill of meeting important English people and seeing her own poems published had all but worn off. She was happy to return to her home in Boston.

On the return trip, Phillis met Abigail Hancock. Hancock had kept Phillis company for part of the trip. They talked about books and all that was happening in Boston—especially the chance of war between England and its American colonies. Both women agreed with the leaders of the colonies—America should seek its independence from England.

7

Two black men hurried ahead of Hancock carrying her wooden clothing trunk. One of the men slipped on a rope and dropped his end on the dock. "Careful!" Hancock shouted as she knocked the man on the head with her book. "My mirror is in there!" The man said he was sorry as he picked up the trunk. Phillis was very sad to see anyone treated so poorly. Yet she knew that if she tried to stop Hancock, it could mean trouble. Phillis, although now a published poet, was still a slave. White people in America enjoyed her company, but that didn't mean they wanted a slave to tell them how to live their lives.

While in England, Wheatley had her first book of poetry published. She was treated as a famous person in England. Although Wheatley was used to being treated better than other slaves in Boston, she was not used to being treated like someone who was famous.

Wheatley was glad to be home again in Boston. Yet something inside her had changed.

In England, she was treated with respect. It had been almost too easy for her to forget that she was someone's property. She had returned because her owner, Susannah Wheatley, was very sick. Mrs. Wheatley had been very kind to Phillis and had treated her like a daughter. She did not allow Phillis to be friends with other slaves, though. Phillis had been allowed to do many things that other black people could not. Still, she wondered when she would be able to walk the streets as free as white people.

On this August day, Boston was buzzing with activity. Just before Phillis had left for London, the British government passed the Tea Act. This law stated that only one company could sell tea in the colonies. The people of Boston, however, said they would not buy the tea. Now dozens of ships loaded with unsold British tea filled Boston Harbor. Some ships had been sitting there when Phillis left for London. Many people in Boston felt that war between England and the colonies was right around the corner.

When Phillis Wheatley was first published, many people did not believe that a slave could write such beautiful poetry. A group of men tested Phillis to see if she really did write her poems. They agreed that she was the author after the test.

Chapter Two

FREE AT LAST

Susannah Wheatley's room was dark and stuffy. The shades were drawn, and a single candle burned on the table by the bed. Her breathing was heavy, but Phillis could tell that she was awake.

"Phillis," Mrs. Wheatley said weakly. "You came home early. Did you like London?"

Phillis went to Mrs. Wheatley's side and took her hand. "I heard you were ill," said Phillis. "I came as soon as I could. I wasn't even able to bring home any copies of my book."

Mrs. Wheatley drew in a quick breath and smiled. "Your book! I knew you could do it. I knew that when you had your first poem published six years ago that you would become a great writer. And now look what has happened. You're only twenty and already you have your own book of poetry."

"Thanks to you, ma'am," Phillis responded.

Angry shouts from Kings Street drifted into the room. The two women sat in silence listening to the fighting between colonists and British soldiers. "That happens more and more lately," Mrs. Wheatley whispered. "I'm afraid there will be a war soon, Phillis."

"Perhaps that is for the best, Ma'am," Phillis said. "The colonists should get their independence from England."

Phillis wondered how the colonists could want their freedom from England, yet keep slaves at the same time. She wanted to ask Mrs. Wheatley why people who loved their freedom so much kept others in chains. However, she remained silent so she would not upset Mrs. Wheatley.

"I'm just so happy that you're home," said Mrs. Wheatley. "Hearing about your trip and your book has brought my strength back." She sat up and grasped Phillis's hands in her own. "You are so special to Mr. Wheatley and I. You are such a big help around the house."

Mrs. Wheatley fell silent for a moment. It was as if she could not bring herself to say what she really wanted to say. "You've been almost like a daughter to us." The sickly woman fell back to her pillow and looked toward the window.

Finally, she said, "We are granting you your freedom, Phillis. You're the second woman in the colonies to get published. And, more importantly, you're the first black person from this country to get published. You were born to be a poet, Phillis, not a slave."

Phillis's eyes filled with tears. A great weight had been lifted from her heart, yet she was filled with worry. "But what will you do without me?" she asked. Mrs. Wheatley told Phillis that she and her husband would be fine.

Phillis thought to herself, *But what will I do without them?* She didn't know where she would go. She had almost no money. Phillis was glad not to be a slave, but now that she was free, what would she do?

THIS DAY IS PUBLISHED

n'd with an elegant Engraving of the

[Price 3s. 4d. L. M. Bud]

POEMS,

n various subjects,—— Religious and Moral.

By PHILLIS WHEATLEY,

A Negro Girl.

Sold by Mess'rs COX & BERRY,

At their Store in King Street, Boston.

The Subscribers are requested to

Copies.

Phillis Wheatley put notices in the local newspapers to sell her books. Some people would pay her for a copy of the book before it was even published.

Chapter Three

ON HER OWN

June 21, 1774

A warm breeze flicked the pages of the book in Phillis's hand. She was trying to write poetry. Yet lately, all she could think about was Susannah Wheatley. Mrs. Wheatley had passed away in March. Her illness had carried on for months. She spent most of that time in her bed. Phillis had stayed by her side like a good friend, feeding her, reading to her, and watching her sleep.

Phillis was still working for the Wheatleys, taking care of their grandchildren. The Wheatley's daughter, Mary Lathrop, was often too sick to take care of her children. Someday though, the family would no longer need Phillis's help. Then, she would have to manage on her own.

The British had closed off Boston Harbor to show that they would not allow the colonies to

become independent. Phillis's books had arrived from England just one week before the British stopped ships from entering or leaving the harbor. Hoping to sell her book, she had placed notices in many local newspapers. People liked her writing. Some of the richest people in town invited Phillis to their homes to read her poetry. Phillis enjoyed sharing her poetry, but some of the people did not treat her with respect because she was a black woman. Some of them could not believe that a former slave could actually write such beautiful poetry.

Still, Phillis sold almost all three hundred copies of her book that the publisher had sent. She waited for more copies to arrive from London. *With the British ships blocking the harbor*, Phillis thought, *that may never happen.*

Mr. Wheatley was preparing to leave Boston in case there was a war, but Phillis did not want to leave. George Washington had recently been selected as the commander of the American Continental army. Phillis had read much about

Washington. She thought that he could help the colonists win the war against the British. Washington was even interested in allowing blacks to join the Continental army. Other leaders did not agree with him. They said that slaves would join the army because it would give them a chance to run away. *And why shouldn't they?* Phillis wondered.

Phillis had few friends who would be able to help her when she was on her own. Although many white people loved her poetry, few wanted to accept her because she had once been a slave. Since the British had blocked the harbor, food and supplies could not get to the colonists. People in the city were beginning to run out of food. Many people did not have money. Phillis wondered how she would be able to take care of herself if she could not sell her book. Phillis looked at the book she held in her hand. There was one thing of which she was sure—she would never give up her poetry.

George Washington (on horse) treated Phillis as an equal when he invited her to come visit him at his winter camp, which was similar to the one in this painting. Still, Washington owned many slaves at his home in Virginia.

Chapter Four

A Quiet Life in Rhode Island

October 25, 1775

The American Revolutionary War began outside of Boston in the towns of Lexington and Concord in April 1775. John Wheatley and Phillis fled to Mary Lathrop's home in Providence, Rhode Island. Like many other homes in Providence, Mary's house had become a resting point for soldiers passing through on their way to the war. The house was always filled with brave young men.

One morning Phillis stood in the yard with a basket of the soldiers' clothes that she had just washed. Her hands were red and raw from washing the clothes all day long. Phillis's best friend, Obour Tanner, stood behind her with a few sheets of paper in her hands. Obour was the only black

person with whom Phillis was close. "Your handwriting looks so beautiful, Phillis. I wish I could write as well as you do," Obour said.

"I've told you a hundred times, Obour. I can teach you to write poetry."

"I know," Obour replied as she read Phillis's words. "But who has time for that? This country is fighting for its freedom." Both women were quiet as they thought about all the slaves who would still not have their freedom after the war.

"Are you really going to send this to General Washington?" Obour asked about Phillis's poem she had just read. The poem told General Washington to keep fighting for the colonies' freedom. If he did, America would win the war.

"Of course I am. Why shouldn't I?" asked Phillis as she worked. She threw damp, heavy sheets over the line while the wind tried to pull them out of her hands. "I'm proud to call myself an American patriot, but there's very little I can do to help my country. I pray that my poem makes General Washington and other

colonists want to fight even harder. Then I'll have done my part in beating the British."

"Everyone knows your life here in the colonies is much better than most slaves' lives," Obour replied. "But I still don't see why you should consider yourself a patriot. You are not treated as an equal by most whites."

Phillis dropped the sheets in her hands and turned to face Obour. "We are Americans just like Mr. Wheatley and George Washington. This country was built with our blood and sweat, and I believe the day will come when all black people will be free—free Americans. After we win the war, General Washington will go on to even greater things. I want him and other leaders to remember that without black slaves, there would be no America."

"I hope you're right, Phillis," Obour replied.

People who sold slaves did not care about the slaves' families. When children were taken from their parents, they would most likely never see them again.

Chapter Five

PHILLIS MEETS WITH GENERAL WASHINGTON

March 20, 1776

The Continental army camp in Cambridge, Massachusetts, was bitter cold. Snow covered the tents, piles of supplies, and even some soldiers who had fallen asleep on the ground near their campfires. Phillis stood in a group of men just outside of George Washington's tent. The men were politicians and military leaders. They occasionally looked over at her shivering in her coat, but no one spoke to her. Phillis didn't mind the weather or the other people. She was just excited that General Washington had written back to her. He had liked her poem so much, that he invited her to pay him a personal visit at his camp.

"Joseph!"

Phillis looked up to see General Washington standing at the opening of his tent. He was much

taller than she had thought he would be. He stood with his hands on his hips and his jaw tightly set as he glanced from her to Joseph Reed, Washington's military secretary.

"Yes, sir?" Reed answered.

"Bring this young lady into my tent at once. And bring her something warm to drink."

Washington led Phillis to a large chair inside his tent. Reed rushed in with a thick blanket and put it over Phillis's shoulders. He placed a cup of hot water in front of her and left.

"Thank you for seeing me so quickly, General Washington. I'm Phillis Wheatley."

Washington made Phillis feel comfortable by asking her about her poetry. He once again praised her talent and thanked her for the great honor.

"Phillis, you've written a wonderful poem about me," said Washington. "You describe me as such an important, strong leader. For that, I thank you. You are a talented writer."

"Thank you, sir," replied Phillis.

"I would like to see this poem published," Washington continued. "But it speaks so

highly of me, I'm afraid people will think I am just trying to make myself look good if it were printed in the newspapers." Phillis was disappointed, but she understood what General Washington was saying.

Phillis asked him about his family life, and he told her about his home in Virginia and his wife, Martha. Occasionally, Washington stopped to give an order to Joseph. Phillis noticed that he could have a conversation with her while running the camp at the same time. Washington began talking about the war and what it meant for the colonies. He talked a lot about freedom. After he had finished, Phillis let him know what she was thinking.

"But sir," Phillis said, and then paused. She nearly changed her mind, but continued with her question. "You own slaves, don't you? How can you speak so strongly about freedom when you own slaves?"

Washington looked out the open flap of his tent. White soldiers sat around fires and soup pots. A black man with a torn jacket and rags on

his feet stood near a few soldiers who were warming themselves by a fire.

"There is no easy answer to your question, Phillis," Washington said. "But your visit today has given me a lot to think about. Now I must go back to the war. Phillis, you are a great voice for all colonists, black and white. I look forward to reading more of your poetry."

Phillis left the general's camp feeling very excited. Phillis thought of how she had been taken from her home when she was only seven and brought to a strange country. Now she was meeting one of the leaders of a new nation. And it had all happened because she had published her poetry.

GLOSSARY

colonies (KOL-uh-neez) territories that have been settled by people from another country and are controlled by that country

colonist (KOL-uh-nist) someone who lives in a newly settled area

equality (I-KWOL-uh-tee) the same rights for everyone

freedom (FREE-duhm) the right to do and say what you like

independence (in-di-PEN-duhnss) the condition of being free from the control of other people

patriot (PAY-tree-uht) someone who loves his or her country and is prepared to fight for it

politicians (pol-uh-TISH-uhnz) people who run for or hold government offices, such as presidents

publish (PUHB-lish) to produce and distribute a book, magazine, newspaper, or any other printed material so that people can buy it

revolution (rev-uh-LOO-shuhn) a violent uprising by the people of a country that changes its system of government

PRIMARY SOURCES

We can learn about the people, places, and events of long ago by studying different sources. These sources include old letters, diaries, maps, drawings, and photographs. For example, look at the drawing of the slave ship on page 29. By analyzing this drawing, we can identify the poor conditions in which slaves had to live while coming to America from Africa. So many slaves were crowded into these ships that many of them died before reaching America.

Other primary sources, such as the letter to Phillis Wheatley from George Washington shown on page 32, help identify the beliefs of people from the past. In the letter, Washington praised Wheatley for being such a good poet, even though he believed in owning slaves. Sources such as the drawing and the letter give us a look at history as it was happening.

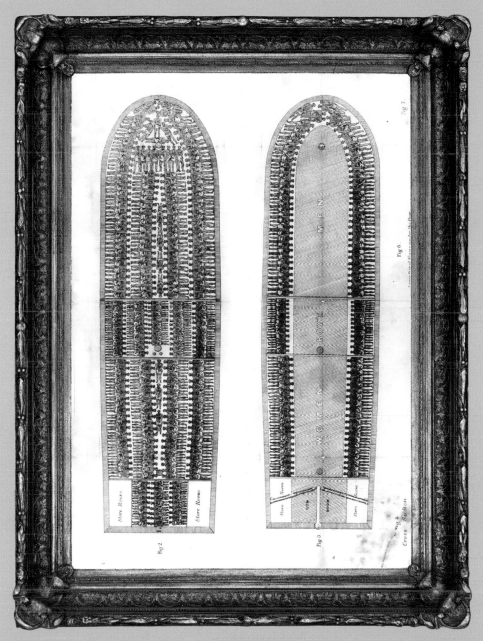

These are plans for a slave ship. The drawing on the left shows how slaves were grouped below the deck of the ship. They were often chained in place for weeks at a time. Many did not survive the journey from Africa.

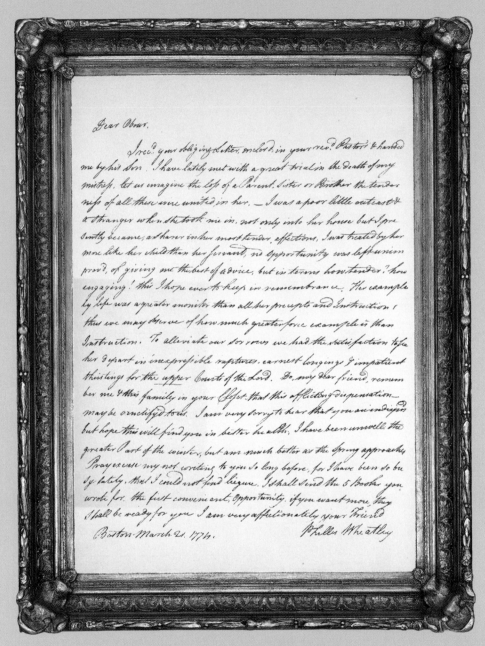

Phillis Wheatley sent this letter to her friend Obour Turner in March 1774. In it, she writes about the death of Susannah Wheatley.

During the Boston Tea Party, colonists dressed up like Native Americans and climbed aboard English tea ships docked in the Boston harbor. They threw all the tea into the harbor to show that they would not pay any more taxes on tea.

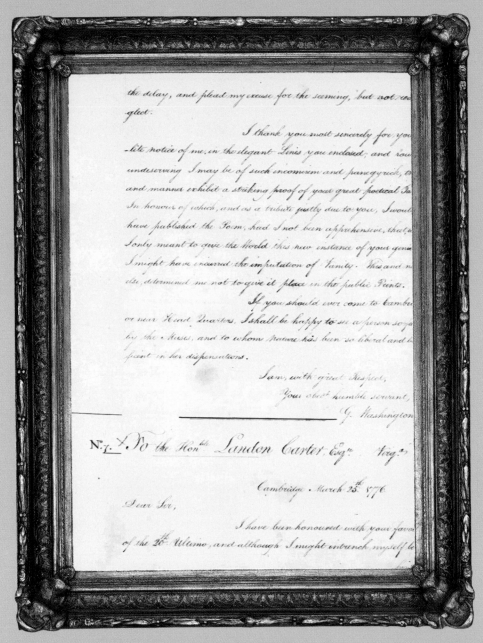

the delay, and plead my excuse for the seeming, but not real neglect.

      I thank you most sincerely for your polite notice of me, in the elegant Lines you enclosed; and however undeserving I may be of such incomium and panegyrick, the style and manner exhibit a striking proof of your great poetical Talents. In honour of which, and as a tribute justly due to you, I would have published the Poem, had I not been apprehensive, that while I only meant to give the World this new instance of your genius, I might have incurred the imputation of Vanity. This and nothing else, determined me not to give it place in the public Prints.

      If you should ever come to Cambridge or near Head Quarters, I shall be happy to see a person so favoured by the Muses, and to whom nature has been so liberal and beneficent in her dispensations.

      I am, with great Respect,
      Your obedt humble servant,
           G. Washington

No. 7. ☓ To the Honble Landon Carter, Esqr. Virga.

      Cambridge. March 25th 776

Dear Sir,

      I have been honoured with your favor of the 20th Ultimo, and although I might intrench myself to

On February 28, 1776, George Washington wrote to Phillis Wheatley. In this letter he thanked her for the poem she wrote about him. He also invited her to visit his camp.